KALEIDOSCOPE

THE BATTLE
OF LITTLE BIGHORN

by
Edward F. Dolan

BENCHMARK BOOKS

MARSHALL CAVENDISH
NEW YORK

Benchmark Books
Marshall Cavendish
99 White Plains Road
Tarrytown, NY 10591
www.marshallcavendish.com

Library of Congress Cataloging-in-Publication Data

Dolan, Edward F., 1924-
The Battle of the Little Bighorn / by Edward F. Dolan.
    p. cm. — (Kaleidoscope)
Includes bibliographical references (p.) and index.
  ISBN 0-7614-1457-6
1. Little Bighorn, Battle of the, Mont., 1876—Juvenile literature. 2. Dakota Indians—Wars—Juvenile literature. I. Title. II.
Kaleidoscope (Tarrytown, N.Y.)
E83.876 .D65 2002
973.8'2—dc21

                                    2002006140

Photo Research by Anne Burns Images

Cover Photo by North Wind Pictures

The photographs in this book are used by permission and through the courtesy of: *North Wind Pictures*: title page, 9, 10, 17, 18, 22, 37; *The Granger Collection,NY*:p. 5, 13, 14, 21, 30, 33, 38, 41; *Corbis*:p. 6 Bettman; *Montana Historical Society*:p. 25; *Little Big Horn Battlefield National Monument*:p. 26 K. F. Roahen Collection;34 Finley Holiday Films;42; *Hulton Archive*:p. 29

Printed in Italy
6 5 4 3 2 1

CONTENTS

The morning of June 25, 1876, was dawning. Lieutenant Colonel George Armstrong Custer led his cavalry troop along the Little Bighorn River in the Montana Territory. He was planning to attack an Indian camp that his scouts had sighted in the far distance.

Custer's troop—the Seventh Cavalry—was part of an army force searching for a large group of runaway Sioux and Cheyenne Indians. On finding them, Custer was to force them to return to the Great Sioux Reservation.

The Indians called Lieutenant Colonel George Armstrong Custer by several nicknames. Two of the best known are Yellow Hair and Long-Haired Man.

Seven years earlier in 1868, the United States had created the reservation in a treaty with Sioux and Cheyenne leaders. It covered thousands of square miles in the present-day states of South Dakota and North Dakota. It was meant to be a home for the two tribes forever.

But many of the Sioux and Cheyenne hated the treaty and never thought of the reservation as their home. And so they went west and settled on open land in the present-day states of Wyoming and Montana.

General William Tecumseh Sherman sits in conference with tribal chiefs before signing the 1868 treaty that created the Great Sioux Reservation. Sherman won fame as a Union Army commander in the Civil War.

The U.S. government left them alone for several years. But then, in 1874, the nation learned that gold had been found in the Black Hills area of the Great Sioux Reservation. Immediately, a flood of white settlers began to pour into the region.

This drawing of the gold-mining camp that became Deadwood City was made as prospectors poured into the Black Hills area of the Great Sioux Reservation in the 1870s.

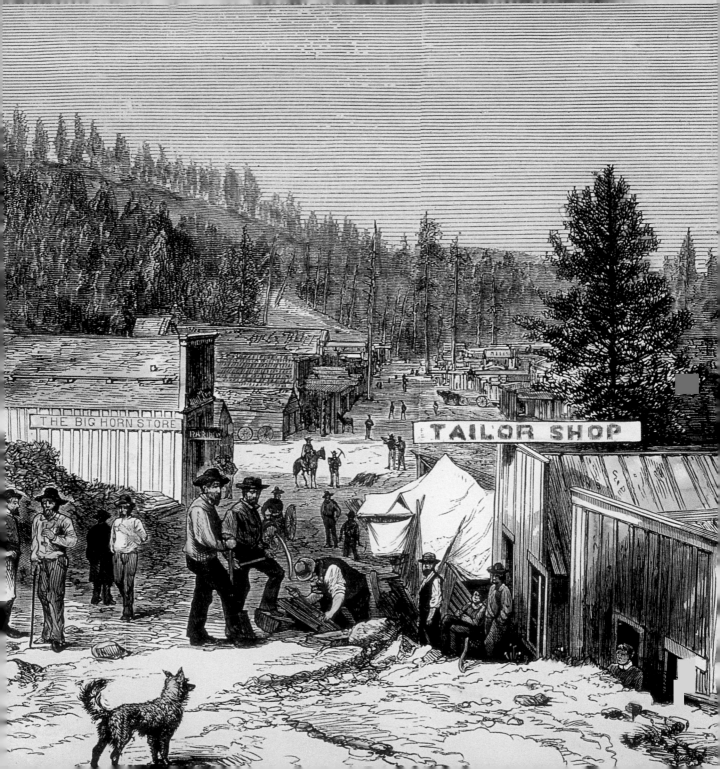

Trouble came swiftly in the wake of the discovery of gold. In the 1868 treaty, the United States had promised to keep the reservation free of outsiders. But now, as white settlers came pouring in, Washington ignored its promise and enraged the Indians on two counts. First, the outsiders were being allowed to violate lands that had long been held to be sacred. Second, the U.S. was beginning to push for treaty changes that would ease the way for even more newcomers.

More and more white settlers began occupying what was considered sacred land to Native Americans. This often let to confrontations between the two groups.

Angry at the broken promise, many Sioux and Cheyenne fled the reservation and hurried west to join their friends in Wyoming and Montana. The move angered the government. In December 1875, it ordered all the runaway Indians to return to the reservation.

They were to return by the end of January 1876. If they failed to do so, the army would hunt them down and return them by force.

Sioux horsemen are seen in a 1903 photograph as they prepare to leave a camp in Nebraska. Many of them were the sons of braves who fought at Little Bighorn.

When the Sioux and Cheyenne failed to appear back at the reservation on the deadline date, the army sent three units to track them down. They were to be arrested and brought back to the reservation. The runaways were suspected of living in the region of the Little Bighorn River in Montana, so the units planned to close in on the areas from different directions.

In this lithograph, U.S. cavalrymen pursue two braves in an effort to return them to the Great Sioux Reservation.

Troops under General George Crook would march north from present-day Wyoming. Next, Colonel John Gibbon would lead a force eastward from Montana. The third group, commanded by General Alfred Terry, would hurry westward from North Dakota.

Marching with Terry was Colonel George Custer's Seventh Cavalry, with more than six hundred men. Custer himself was one of the most famous officers in the army. His exploits during the Civil War had won him the rank of major general when he was just twenty-three years old—making him the army's youngest general. He was now in his mid-thirties.

Custer leads his Seventh Cavalry in a wintertime search for runaway Sioux and Cheyenne. The search ended on June 25, 1876, on the banks of the Greasy Grass River, the Indian name for the Little Bighorn.

17

The three units began to move in the spring of 1876, but General Crook's one thousand troops soon ran into trouble. On June 16, fifteen hundred warriors under Chief Crazy Horse attacked as the Americans were advancing north toward the Little Bighorn River. The two forces battled for six hours, until both withdrew. Crook returned to his home base to the south, and called off his search because his men were so exhausted.

Sioux warriors under Crazy Horse charge General George Crook's men during the six-hour battle that stopped his advance on the Little Bighorn. The general, who was nicknamed Gray Fox by the Indians, later led troops in action against the Apache warrior Geronimo.

Fifty miles to Crook's north, General Terry and Colonel Gibbon finally sighted each other. They came together at a point on the Yellowstone River. There they received word that scouts had sighted a Sioux and Cheyenne trail heading in the direction of the nearby Little Bighorn. The two officers felt sure that the Indians would make camp somewhere along the river. But where? And how big would the camp be? No one could say.

The American troops advanced on the Little Bighorn from different directions. General John Gibbon (right) and his men marched in from the east, where they had been stationed at Fort Ellis in Montana.

THE PLAN OF ATTACK

General Terry quickly worked out a plan of attack. All the troops—except Custer's Seventh Calvary—would search along the Little Bighorn and then strike the camp from the north when it was sighted. Custer, however, would continue on a short distance farther south. When he finally stopped, he would station his troops so that they could cut off any Indian attempt to flee in that direction. He would then await the arrival of General Terry and Colonel Gibbon or, if it seemed necessary, attack the village on his own.

White and Native-American scouts marched with the troops to search out Indian tracks. Though not seen in this pen-and-ink sketch, the Indian scouts were among Custer's most trusted men. On sighting the giant encampment on the Little Bighorn, one of his favorite scouts, Bloody Knife, reported that there were more warriors ahead than the bullets carried by his soldiers.

23

Early on June 25, Custer's scouts brought him word that the camp had been sighted. He was now well to its south, and he decided not to wait for the arrival of Terry and Gibbon. He would attack immediately. It was a move that would cost him his life.

Custer had no idea of the camp's size. It stretched for about two miles along the river. It consisted of some one thousand lodges that housed approximately seven thousand men, women, and children. Between one thousand and two thousand of their number were warriors, under the leadership of Chiefs Sitting Bull, Crazy Horse, Low Dog, and others.

Seen here is an Indian camp that was once photographed alongside the Little Bighorn. The camp on that fatal day in 1876 must have looked like this—but vastly larger.

26

THE ATTACK

Custer took action by first ordering one of his officers, Captain Frederick Benteen, to move toward the southern edge of the camp with about two hundred men. There, Benteen would keep the Indians from escaping in that direction.

Next, Custer marched north toward the camp. Riding alongside him was Major Marcus A. Reno, his second-in-command. As they neared their destination, they saw hundreds of Indians dash out of their dwellings, preparing to fight. Custer ordered Reno to charge the camp with some two hundred men. At the same time,

When Major Marcus A. Reno (left) charged into the Indian camp, his men were quickly forced back. At first, they tried to fight on foot, but they soon had to take cover in a stand of trees. Then they charged through the attacking Indians and made their way to a bluff across the river.

27

Custer and 264 troopers swung away and took shelter behind a line of low hills. They then worked their way past the camp so that they could attack it from the north. They did not foresee the coming disaster.

The Indians forced Major Reno and his men back when they attempted to follow Custer's orders. Reno finally took up a defensive position on a bluff overlooking the Little Bighorn. There, Benteen's contingent joined him. The two officers then fought off repeated enemy attacks for two days. The fighting finally cost them about fifty men killed and sixty wounded out of their total force of four hundred.

This painting shows Major Reno and his soldiers galloping to the bluff where, with Captain Benteen's men, they held off an Indian attack for two days. Months later—in 1879—Reno faced a military trial on charges of cowardice for not fighting his way to Custer's side. He was eventually cleared of the accusations.

But a greater tragedy befell Custer. As he and his men approached the camp late in the afternoon, a force of 2,500 Indian warriors suddenly swept in on them. Amid the shots from the Indians' rifles, the Americans retreated up a hillside. But, once there, they found themselves pinned down by the Indian fire. One by one, the members of the Seventh Cavalry lost their lives. Within an hour, none of Custer's 264 men was still alive.

This lithograph dramatically captures the final moments in the lives of Custer and his Seventh Cavalry. Custer and all 264 of his men were killed in less than an hour.

The details of how Custer and his men died have remained something of a mystery ever since. The attacking braves were the only living witnesses, and most of them chose to remain silent, or to say little of what had happened that late afternoon. Many feared that, if they told their stories, the U.S. government would punish them.

It was rumored, however, that Custer himself died at the hands of a Sioux warrior named One Bull, who was the adopted son of Sitting Bull. One Bull never admitted to the killing.

This pictograph was painted in 1881 by Red Horse, a Sioux chief who participated in the Little Bighorn fighting. It shows Custer and his men meeting their deaths.

33

When General Terry and Colonel Gibbon arrived on the scene, the attack on Benteen's and Reno's men finally came to an end. The Sioux and Cheyenne warriors retreated into the distance, taking their families with them.

In this painting, the artist depicts the departure of the victorious Sioux and Cheyenne from Little Bighorn. They carried their dead and wounded away with them. Before leaving, they stripped equipment, arms, and ammunition from the American dead.

The two commanding officers immediately visited the hillside where Custer and his troops had died. They found the men sprawled everywhere, dust and blood covering their bodies. General Terry ordered that they be carefully buried where they had fallen. The Indians who had died in the battle were gone—their families had carried away their bodies.

The white markers in this present-day photograph of the Little Bighorn battlefield show where American soldiers' bodies were found.

The news of what had happened that June day reached the outside world within a few weeks. A wave of anger spread throughout the United States. It was accompanied by a cry of outrage from the public and the army. Both demanded that the Indians be punished for the deaths in what newspapers everywhere were soon calling "Custer's Last Stand."

More than one thousand drawings and paintings of the Battle of Little Bighorn have been made by American artists. One of the best known is this one, painted in the late 1800s by Cassily Adams.

The next few years were disastrous ones for the Sioux and Cheyenne. Both tribes suffered defeats in the battles that followed when army troops, seeking revenge, sought them out. Chief Crazy Horse and his followers fought until 1877, when starvation forced them to surrender. He was then stabbed to death in a military prison. Chief Sitting Bull and his followers fled to Canada and hunted buffalo until 1881. On returning to the United States, he lived on a reservation and spent some time as a star performer in Buffalo Bill Cody's Wild West Show. The chief was killed by Indian police during a period of tribal unrest in 1890.

Chief Sitting Bull ranks as one of the most important Indian leaders at Little Bighorn. Following the battle, he led his people to safety in Canada. He also traveled for a time with William "Buffalo Bill" Cody's Western show. The chief is seen here with Cody in an 1885 photograph taken in Montreal, Canada.

BVT. MAJ. GEN'L G. A. CUSTER.

CAPTAINS.
M. W. KEOGH.
G. W. YATES.
T. W. CUSTER.

LIEUTENANTS.
W. W. COOK.
A. E. SMITH.
DONALD McINTOSH.
JAMES CALHOUN.
J. E. PORTER.
B. H. HODGSON.
J. C. STURGIS.
W. VAN W. REILY.
J. J. CRITTENDEN.
H. M. HARRINGTON.

ASSISTANT SURGEONS.
G. E. LORD.   J. M. DE WOLF.

SOLDIERS.

W. H. SHARROW.	GEO. EISEMAN.
JAMES DALIOUS.	GUSTAVE ENGLE.
J. E. ARMSTRONG.	JAMES FARRAND.
JAMES DRINAN.	PAT'K GRIFFIN.
JAMES McDONALD.	JAMES HATHERSALL.
RICH'D ROLLINS.	ALPHEUS STUART.
JNO. SULLIVAN.	IGNATZ STUNGWITZ.
T. P. SWEETSER.	LUDWIG ST. JOHN.
RICH'D DORN.	GARRETT VAN ALLEN.
JERE. FINLEY.	O. F. WARNER.
AUGUST FINCKLE.	HENRY WYMAN.
T. J. BUCKNELL.	CHAS. VINCENT.
WM. KRAMER.	PAT'K GOLDEN.
GEO. HOWELL.	EDW'D HOUSEN.
JNO. BRIGHTFIELD.	FRED'N HOHMEYER.
CHRISTOPHER CRIDDLE.	RICH'D FARRELL.

IN MEMORY OF
OFFICERS AND SOLDIERS WHO FELL NEAR THIS PLACE,
FIGHTING WITH THE 7TH UNITED STATES CAVALRY
AGAINST SIOUX INDIANS
ON THE 25TH AND 26TH OF JUNE
A.D. 1876.

The Battle of Little Bighorn is now considered the beginning of the end of the wars in which America's original people valiantly fought to protect their lands from an ever-growing white population. The struggle finally came to an end in the last days before the dawn of the twentieth century.

A monument to the Seventh Cavalry sits atop a mass grave at the Little Bighorn battlefield. This photograph was taken in 1885.

1868–1875

The United States establishes the Great Sioux Reservation in what is now South Dakota and North Dakota.

December 1875

The United States orders runaway Indians to return to the reservation by the following January.

Spring 1876

The army sends three cavalry units to find the runaway Indians, who are thought to be near the Little Bighorn River in Montana. On the way to the river, one of the cavalry units is attacked by Indians and returns to its base camp.

June 1876

Colonel George Custer, commanding the Seventh Cavalry, learns a large party of Indians has been sighted alongside the Little Bighorn.

June 25, morning

Custer advances toward the Indian camp. He divides his men into three groups. He will personally lead one of the groups.

June 25, afternoon

While Custer's group is working its way around the camp, the Indians attack the other two units. The two successfully fight off the attackers until help arrives two days later.

June 25, late afternoon

A force of 2,500 braves attacks Custer's group as he approaches the camp. He and the 264 men with him lose their lives in less than one hour.

FIND OUT MORE

BOOKS

Avery, Susan and Linda Skinner. *Extraordinary American Indians*. Chicago: Children's Press, 1992.

Carnes, Mark C., and John A. Garraty, with Patrick Williams. *Mapping America's Past: A Historical Atlas*. New York: Henry Holt, 1996.

Hirschfelder, Arlene. *Native Americans: A History in Pictures*. New York: Dorling Kindersley Publishing, 2000.

Viola, Herman J. *Little Bighorn Remembered: The Untold Indian Story of Custer's Last Stand*. New York: Times Books, 1999.

AUTHOR'S BIO

Edward F. Dolan is the author of over one hundred nonfiction books for young people and adults. He has written on medicine and science, law, history, folklore, and current social issues. Mr. Dolan is a native Californian, born in the San Francisco region and raised in Southern California. In addition to writing books, he has been a newspaper reporter and a magazine editor. He currently lives in the northern part of the state.

INDEX

Page numbers for illustrations are in boldface.